£1·50

SOUTH DEVON COAST FROM THE AIR

Published titles in this series:

Somerset Coast from the Air
North Devon Coast from the Air
North Cornwall Coast from the Air
South Cornwall Coast from the Air
Dorset Coast from the Air

Forthcoming titles in this series:

Hampshire Coast from the Air
Isle of Wight from the Air
Sussex Coast from the Air
Essex Coast from the Air
Kent Coast from the Air

SOUTH DEVON COAST
from the Air

PHOTOGRAPHY BY JASON HAWKES

HALSGROVE

First published in Great Britain in 2008

Copyright © in this publication Halsgrove 2008
Images by Jason Hawkes

All rights reserved. No part of this publication may be reproduced, stored in a retrieval system, or transmitted in any form or by any means without the prior permission of the copyright holder.

British Library Cataloguing-in-Publication Data
A CIP record for this title is available from the British Library

ISBN 978 1 84114 678 2

HALSGROVE
Halsgrove House, Ryelands Industrial Estate
Bagley Road, Wellington, Somerset TA21 9PZ
t: 01823 653777 f: 01823 216796
e: sales@halsgrove.com   www.halsgrove.com

Printed and bound by D'Auria Industrie Grafiche Spa, Italy

INTRODUCTION

Devon is unique among English counties in having two separated coastlines. That each coastline is as different as chalk from cheese is amply revealed through the photographs in this book and its sister publication *North Devon Coast from the Air*. It might be imagined that while North Devon's lofty and rugged cliffs were built to withstand the fury of the Atlantic Ocean, the southern coastline is more gently inclined towards the calmer waters of the English Channel.

Devon's south coast provides more natural shelter than the north and all along the southern shore are safe harbours around which, from ancient times, fishing communities established themselves. It is towards this shore that most of Devon's rivers run, creating deep tidal valleys. These days some of the most desirable and expensive homes in Britain are to be found here. And where fishing boats once tied up alongside granite harbour walls, yachts now lay up at pontoons or rock gently at vast marinas.

In this book we are taken on an aerial journey along the South Devon coast starting at Plymouth and heading east for some 115 miles (184km) where we reach the Dorset border. All along the coast are echoes of Devon's proud maritime heritage, anchorages from where the Pilgrim Fathers last set foot on English soil and from whence the likes of Ralegh, Drake and Hawkins sailed out to fame and fortune. The mouths of the rivers Plym, Dart and Exe were also the routes through which Britain grew to one of the greatest trading nations the world has ever seen, backed by her naval power that often sailed from Devon ports to keep the rest of the world in thrall.

These days, the coastline provides the means for thousands to enjoy leisure pursuits. The South West Coast Path follows the cliff edge for most of its route through South Devon, while sandy beaches are thronged in summer months providing safe bathing, in most places, while easy access provides a chance to explore harbourside towns and villages.

The principal attraction of aerial photographs is that they are literally a bird's-eye view, allowing us to look down on the landscape from a perspective that we never normally see. Such pictures reveal to us things that are normally hidden from view, and often surprise us when we find that what we had imagined the layout of the land to be is in reality quite different. The best practitioners of this genre of photography also strive to capture an aesthetic in the images they take, and these pictures, sometimes quite abstract in appearance, are often strikingly beautiful in their own right.

Jason Hawkes is one of the country's best-known photographers specialising in aerial photography. From his base near London he travels worldwide to produce images for books, advertising and design. Since 1991 he has provided photographs for major international companies including Nike, HSBC, Ford, Rolex, Toyota and BP. The images in this book and the sister publications in the series were specially commissioned by Halsgrove.

For more information regarding Jason Hawkes' work visit www.jasonhawkes.com. For a complete list of titles in this series and other Halsgrove titles visit www.halsgrove.com.

Looking north over Plymouth, one of Britain's greatest naval ports and with a rich maritime heritage. The Hoe, on which Sir Francis Drake is said to have played a game of bowls before setting out to defeat the Spanish Armada, is bathed in sunlight.

Left: On the left of the photograph lies the Cattewater and, winding its way northward, the River Plym from which the city takes its name. Turnchapel rises in the foreground with Hooe, Hexton, Oreston and Plymstock beyond. The tide has receded from Hooe Lake (right foreground). *Above:* Near the Marine Centre at the mouth of the River Yealm, with the outskirts of Wembury just seen on the left.

Previous page: Newton Ferrers nestles in the sweep of the River Yealm, with Dartmoor's hills far distant.

Left: Low tide: Newton Ferrers from the Noss Mayo side of the creek.

Above: Late summer fields along the clifftop at Erme Mouth.

Previous page: Looking south towards Bigbury Bay from the Erme estuary.

Above: The famous Art Deco hotel on Burgh Island was built in 1929 and has connections with many famous celebrities including Noel Coward and Agatha Christie.

Right: Looking across Burgh Island to Bigbury-on-Sea (left) and towards the mouth of the River Avon, with Thurlestone in the middle distance.

Left: A magnificent view westwards down the coast from Burgh Island with Bigbury on the mainland and the holiday park beyond. The spit of sand linking the island to the shore is covered as the tide comes in but the island remains accessible through the use of a special high-rise tractor.

Left: The village of Thurlestone is separated from the sea by the local golf course alongside which runs the South Devon Coast Path.

Above: A little to the east of the village, Thurlestone Sands offer visitors tranquility and relative seclusion.

Previous page: The villages of Outer Hope (near foreground) and Inner Hope (distant), nestling around Hope Cove.

Left and above: Being a little off the beaten track, Hope Cove seems to avoid too much overcrowding and locals enjoy its relative seclusion both in summer and for winter walks.

Above and right: From Bolt Tail to Bolt Head this stretch of the South Devon coast offers endless opportunities for recreation, from building sandcastles to watersports.

Previous page: South Sands lies at the mouth of Salcombe Harbour.

Above: Sandy coves on both sides of the inlet to Salcombe Harbour attract sailors and sunbathers.

Above: A simply magnificent view over Salcombe Harbour looking towards the town, with Bolt Head in the distance.

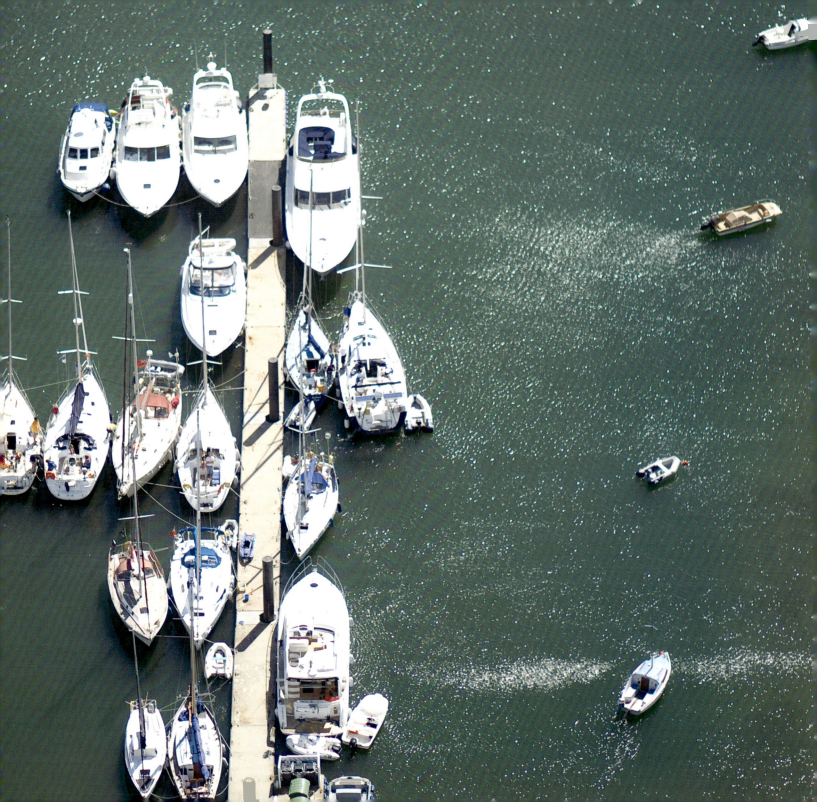

Left and above: Salcombe Harbour – the perfect place for yachties and boaties of every kind.

Above: Salcombe, where you can simply step off your boat and into the centre of the town.

Right: A busy cove opposite Salcombe just below the village of East Portlemouth.

Left and above: Superb cliffwalking is on offer around Prawle Point – and there's always something to see.

Above: Shipwreck! A reminder that these cliffs can be dangerous too, especially in winter months with onshore gales.

Right: The Coastguard Station at Prawle Point.

Previous page: Near Langerstone Point looking west down the coast, with Prawle Point on the left and the village of East Prawle glimpsed on the right.

Left: Farmland comes down to the edge of the sea. East Prawle and the hinterland of the South Hams beyond.

Above: Start Point, the most southerly point of the British Isles, at the entrance to Start Bay.

Left: Start Point lighthouse was built in 1836.

Above: Hallsands. This is the village that was famously lost to the sea, swept away by storms in the early part of the last century.

Previous page: The wonderful sweep of the Devon countryside beyond the beach at Beesands.

Left: Torcross and the sandbank that encloses the freshwater lake of Slapton Lea.

Above: Many locals would confess to Blackpool Sands being their favourite beach on this stretch of coast, and you can see why.

Previous page: Packed with history, blessed with unparalleled beauty, a breathtaking view of the harbour at Dartmouth.

Above: Dartmouth Royal Naval College.

Left: Dartmouth, looking seawards.

Previous page: A view over Dartmouth towards Kingswear which lies on the opposite side of the harbour.

Left: The Quay, Dartmouth. One of the safest deep anchorages in Britain, the harbour can accommodate vessels of every type.

Above: Kinsgwear. The railway ended here when early plans to bridge the River Dart, mercifully, were never completed.

Above: Looking down on South Embankment, Dartmouth.

Right: Warfleet Road, Dartmouth, winds alongside some of the most desirable riverside properties in Britain.

Previous page: The breakwater at Brixham points like a finger towards the heart of Tor Bay.

Left: Brixham harbour and town, from the east.

Above: Goodrington Sands, one of Torbay's most popular beaches.

Previous page: A marvellous view over Roundham Head towards Paignton, with Paignton harbour on the right.

Left: The pier and esplanade at Paignton looking into the centre of the town.

Above: Torquay and the harbour, with Babbacombe Bay in the distance.

Left: Hesketh Crescent and Meadfoot recapture the elegance of Victorian Torquay.

Above: More modern developments take advantage of views across the bay.

Right: Anstey's Cove, and Babbacombe beyond.

Left: A speedboat circles off Oddicombe Beach to where a cliff railway carries people from St Marychurch above. On the left the view extends back over Torquay to Paignton and Brixham beyond.

Previous page: East of Tor Bay is Babbacombe Bay – here looking towards Maidencombe across an emerald sea.

Left: A magnificent view up the River Teign, with Shaldon on the left and Teignmouth, with its famous pier, on the right.

Above: The Salty forms a natural little harbour, with the houses of Teignmouth sitting alongside.

Above: Shaldon, across the estuary from Teignmouth, has always enjoyed the reputation of quiet gentility. *Right:* This whole coastline offers perfect havens for sailing types.

Previous page: The Salty, looking out to sea.

Left: Shaldon's main street, The Strand, runs right alongside the seafront. *Above:* The Salty is perfect for holidaymakers but the narrow estuary entrance requires constant dredging and much skill is required to bring larger vessels into Teignmouth Harbour.

Left: Safe bathing and an ideal place for building sandcastles, the seafront at Teignmouth. *Above:* A dramatic bird's-eye view over The Parson and Clerk, a rock formation between Teignmouth and Dawlish said to resemble two such figures.

Previous page: Dawlish is familiar to thousands who travel to the westcountry by train, as the railway runs along the seafront here. The town itself has many elegant houses.

Left: Dawlish grew to prominence as a Victorian watering place, encouraged by easy access via the Great Western Railway.

Above: Dawlish Warren, a favourite summer playground, is formed by a sandspit that extends into the Exe estuary.

Previous page: A superb panoramic view of the Exe estuary with Exeter in the far distance, the last of Dawlish Warren's sandspit on the left, and Exmouth on the right.

Left: A summer's day and a cricket match is underway on The Maer, Exmouth.

Above: These red cliffs are a striking feature of the coast between Exmouth and Budleigh Salterton.

Previous page: Looking north over Budleigh Salterton with Woodbury Common on the near horizon.

Above: Looking west from the direction of Lympstone back down the Devon coast, with Exmouth on the left extending into the Exe, coming almost to meet Dawlish Warren mid-estuary.

Left: A spectacular vista with Budleigh Salterton in the near foreground and Sandy Bay and Exmouth beyond.

Previous page: Looking over Topsham towards Exminster, with the Exeter Canal winding its way along the side of the Exe estuary and the Dartmoor hills far distant.

Left: Lympstone on the River Exe.

Above: Looking into Exmouth Dock. Once a busy commercial port it is now largely given over to leisure craft.

Previous page: Exmouth, looking north towards Exeter.

Above: Exmouth from the east looking back over The Maer.

Left: The Esplanade at Exmouth runs along the seafront, skirting sandy beaches.

Left: The Queen's Drive runs along the coast from Exmouth ending abruptly at Orcombe.

Above: From Orcombe the coastline sweeps eastward past Sandy Bay and on towards Budleigh Salterton.

Previous page: East Devon's famous red cliffs. Sandy Bay holiday park dominates the headland.

Left: Hundreds of static caravans leave their mark on the landscape at Sandy Bay.

Above: The Royal Marines firing range at Sandy Bay overlooks an important seabird nesting site.

Above: Looking east to Budleigh Salterton. The River Otter can be seen entering the sea on the right.

Right: Looking west over Budleigh Salterton.

Left and above: Between Budleigh Salterton and Sidmouth. The farmed countryside and the natural shape of the land create almost abstract forms when seen from the air.

Previous page: Ladram Bay near Otterton is another popular holiday park.

Above: Perfectly manicured, the cricket ground and bowling greens at Sidmouth.

Right: The Esplanade, Sidmouth.

Previous page: As with many coastal towns, the threat of erosion is an increasing problem at Sidmouth. Here, where the River Sid enters the sea, a stone breakwater helps prevent erosion.

Left: One of the many public parks in Sidmouth.

Above: A quiet corner at the western end of the beach, Sidmouth.

Previous page: Deckchairs face seaward along the Esplanade, Exmouth.

Above and right: In January 2007 the MSC *Napoli* was holed during a storm and was run aground near Branscombe on the South Devon coast. Posing a danger to wildlife and the environment the wreck was broken up over the following months leaving, at the time these photographs were taken, just the superstructure of the wreck in view.

Previous page: Looking west down the coast towards Sidmouth the village of Branscombe is glimpsed on the right, with the wreck of the *Napoli* just visible offshore

Left: The beach at Branscombe with Seaton Bay just visible beyond.

Above: Red cliffs give way to chalk. Looking east towards Beer with Seaton in the distance.

Previous page: Beer Head.

Left: Beer, once famed for its smugglers, is now a favourite tourist destination.

Right: Looking down on to Fore Street, Beer. Quarries near the village provided stone for many famous buildings and Beer Stone was used in the building of Exeter Cathedral.

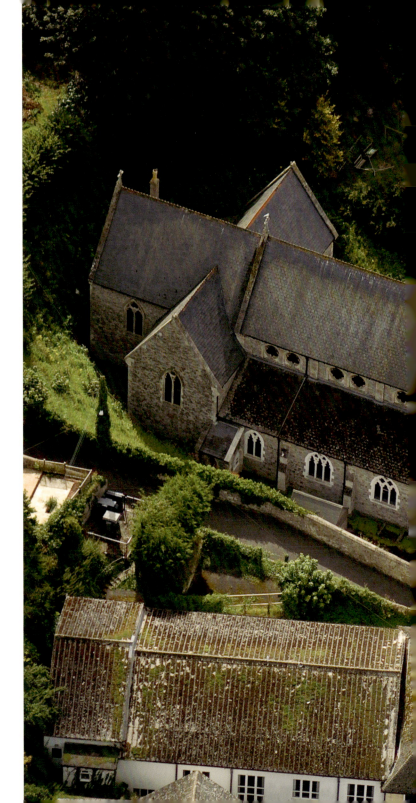

Previous page: The village centre, Beer.

Left and above: Devon relies heavily on tourism and a spell of good weather brings thousands flocking to the beaches of South Devon.

Previous page: The River Axe forms the boundary between Devon and Dorset with Seaton lying just to the west of the river mouth.

Above: The last of Devon: a view westward down the coast towards Seaton and beyond.